W0301311

Jorunn Berntzen & David O'Gorman

Business Vocabulary Elementary

Cornelsen
& OXFORD

Business Vocabulary Elementary wurde geplant und entwickelt von der Verlagsredaktion der Cornelsen und Oxford University Press GmbH, Berlin.

Verfasser: David O'Gorman M.A., Jorunn Berntzen
Verlagsredaktion: James Austin M.A., Elizabeth Alexander
Layout/Herstellung: Sabine Trittin

Erhältlich sind auch: Business Vocabulary Intermediate (Best.-Nr. 27538)
Business Grammar and Vocabulary (Best.-Nr. 24210)
Business Grammar Elementary (Best.-Nr. 27465)
Business Grammar Intermediate (Best.-Nr. 27473)

1. Auflage

5.	4.	3.	2.	1.	Die letzten Ziffern bezeichnen Zahl
2000	1999	1998	1997	1996	und Jahr des Druckes.

Alle Drucke dieser Auflage können, weil untereinander unverändert, im Unterricht nebeneinander verwendet werden.

Bestellnummer 27520

ISBN 3-8109-2752-0

Druck & Weiterverarbeitung: Saladruck
Vertrieb: Cornelsen Verlag, Berlin

Gedruckt auf chlorfrei gebleichtem Papier, ohne Dioxinbelastung der Gewässer.

Vorwort

Liebe Benutzerinnen und Benutzer,

ob Sie sich beim Studium, im Beruf oder in der Freizeit mit Englisch beschäftigen, mit diesem Vokabeltrainer können Sie vor allem Ihre Kenntnisse des Wirtschaftsenglisch festigen. Sie werden nicht nur Ihren Wortschatz üben und erweitern, sondern auch feststellen, daß Ihnen Vokabellernen Freude machen kann und der Erfolg Ihre Mühen lohnen wird.

Business Vocabulary Elementary bietet Ihnen mehr als klassisches Vokabellernen. Nicht das Erlernen einzelner Begriffe, sondern die kontextbezogene Aneignung wichtiger Vokabeln und Redewendungen aus dem Wirtschaftsleben steht im Vordergrund. Die dargestellten Rahmenhandlungen spiegeln authentische Situationen, in denen Sie Ihre Kenntnisse einsetzen werden, wider. Sie durchlaufen die relevanten Abteilungen eines Unternehmens, lernen in Englisch zu telefonieren, Reisen zu planen und zu buchen, sind im Ein- und Verkauf tätig, wickeln Bank- und andere Geschäfte ab. Mit Hilfe des Lösungsteils können Sie überprüfen, ob Sie dies alles in perfektem Englisch bewältigt haben.

Die Vielfalt der Übungen und das Layout des Buches animieren zum Lernen. Die Übungen stammen aus dem praktischen Wirtschaftsleben. Sie trainieren und erweitern den Wortschatz, bauen fundierte Wortfelder auf, trainieren die Übersetzungsfähigkeiten und das logische Denken in der englischen Sprache. Ein Glossar auf fast jeder Seite hilft Ihnen, sich im Bereich Wirtschaftsenglisch rasch einen funktionsfähigen Grundwortschatz anzueignen.

Business Vocabulary Elementary eignet sich für das Selbststudium und kann als Ergänzung zu den weiteren in dieser Reihe erschienenen Lehrwerken **Business Grammar Elementary** und **Business Grammar Intermediate**, **Business Vocabulary Intermediate** und **Business Grammar and Vocabulary** genutzt werden.

Wir wünschen Ihnen viel Erfolg und Freude mit **Business Vocabulary Elementary**.

Berlin, im Juni 1996

Ihre Autoren

Inhalt

The office 1

A Furniture, equipment and stationery

Auf diesem Bild sehen Sie das Büro der Verkaufsabteilung von Fletcher Industries, einer kleinen britischen Firma.

The office contains several pieces of furniture. There are two desks. The one on the left belongs to the sales manager, Mr Charles Dawson. The one on the right belongs to his secretary, Miss Linda Brown. In front of Mr Dawson's desk there are two chairs for visitors. Beside the window, on the left, we can see two filing cabinets. These contain documents about the company's products and customers.

Below the window there is a table. On it there are two pieces of office equipment: a computer and a printer. Next to it is another table with a fax. On the wall, beside the window, there is a chart which shows sales figures. Below this chart, in the corner of the office, we can see a small safe. The sales manager keeps money and important documents here.

Hier sehen Sie den Schreibtisch von Miss Brown.

On the top we can see her computer with its keyboard and monitor. She types Mr Dawson's correspondence on it. She stores data on a disk. She can find information about customers, orders and bills very quickly. She also has a telephone, a diary and a message pad.

Miss Brown's desk has two drawers on the right. Here she keeps her stationery: paper, envelopes, pens and pencils and other things she needs for her work.

Wendungen und Begriffe

furniture	Büroeinrichtung	*sales figures*	Absatzzahlen
equipment	Bürotechnik	*safe*	Safe
stationery	Bürobedarf	*keyboard*	Tastatur
to contain	enthalten	*to store*	speichern
to belong to	gehören zu	*bill*	Rechnung
in front of	vor jdm/etw	*diary*	Terminkalender
filing cabinet	Aktenschrank	*message pad*	Notizblock
chart	Tabelle, Diagramm	*drawer*	Schublade

Übung 1

Vervollständigen Sie die Sätze mit Hilfe der Wörter aus dem Kasten.

stores • contains • keeps • shows • needs • belongs • finds • types

1 The secretary ________________ her paper in the drawers of her desk.

2 The blue car ________________ to the sales manager.

3 Miss Brown ________________ letters on a computer.

4 The picture on page 5 ________________ the furniture in an office.

5 The company ________________ information on computer disks.

6 The office ________________ a lot of furniture and equipment.

7 With a computer, the secretary ________________ information very easily.

8 Miss Brown ________________ a computer to do her job quickly.

Übung 2

Ordnen Sie die Wörter jeweils dem richtigen Oberbegriff zu.

envelopes • desks • printers • pens • filing cabinets • paper • pencils • computer • chairs • tables

Furniture: ______________________________

Stationery: ______________________________

Equipment: ______________________________

Übung 3

Korrigieren Sie diese Sätze über das Büro, das Sie auf der ersten Abbildung sehen.

1 Miss Brown's desk is on the left of the picture.

____

2 The filing cabinets are below the window.

____

3 The safe is in the middle of the office.

____

4 There are two chairs behind Mr Dawson's desk.

____

5 The table is beside the window.

____

6 The sales manager keeps money on top of the safe.

____

7 Miss Brown's message pad is in a drawer in her desk.

____

8 Miss Brown has four drawers on the left of her desk.

____

B Jobs

Miss Brown arrives at the office every day from Monday to Friday at 9 a.m. Mr Dawson sometimes arrives before 8.30 a.m. Usually they both leave at 5 p.m. Mr Dawson often works on Saturdays, too. He is a very busy man.

He is in charge of the sales department, and sells the company's products to customers in Britain and overseas. He has about 500 customers in Britain, and approximately 150 in other countries. He has a staff of six sales representatives in different parts of Britain, and he sells to agents in Germany, France, Switzerland and Italy.

He deals with customers' orders and supplies them with the goods they need. He also occasionally handles complaints. Sometimes he receives orders through his sales representatives and agents, and sometimes customers contact him direct by telephone or fax.

Mr Dawson's secretary, Linda Brown, helps him in several ways. She takes telephone messages for him. She writes letters to customers. She receives visitors to the office, and makes appointments for people who want to talk to him. When Mr Dawson is abroad, Miss Brown does some of his work.

Wendungen und Begriffe

to be in charge of	verantwortlich sein	*to handle*	sich befassen mit
approximately	ungefähr, etwa	*complaint*	Reklamation, Beschwerde
staff	Mitarbeiterstab	*message*	Mitteilung, Nachricht
sales representative	Vertreter(in)	*to make an appointment*	ein Termin vereinbaren
to deal with	zuständig sein für, sich kümmern um	*abroad*	im Ausland
to supply	beliefern		
occasionally	gelegentlich		

Übung 4

Finden Sie die Entsprechung zu folgenden Ausdrücken und Wendungen im Text.

1 Now and again

____

2 Responsible for

____

3 People who buy things

____

4 In other countries

____

5 All the people working for a company or department

____

6 A person who represents a company in a foreign country

____

7 Arrangements to meet people

____

Übung 5

Lesen Sie sich beide Texte noch einmal durch, und ordnen Sie die Wörter sinngemäß in drei Gruppen ein.

occasionally • often • computer • keyboard • usually •
disk • store • contain • sometimes • keep • monitor • hold

________	________	________
________	________	________
________	________	________
________	________	________

2 The company

A The site

Schauen Sie sich den Lageplan von Fletcher Industries an.

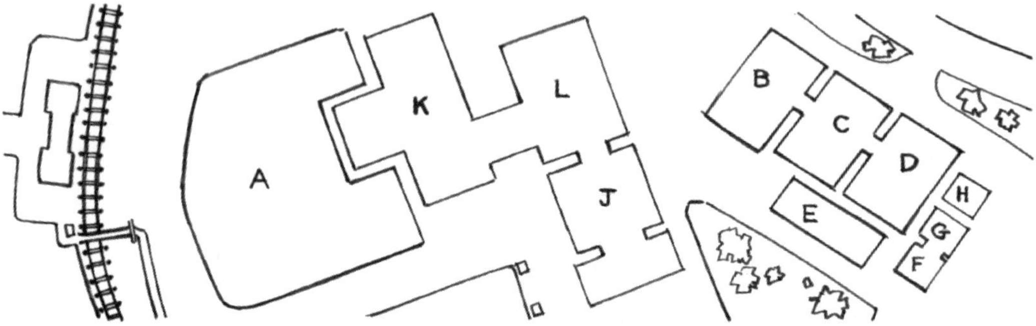

The site is located near a railway station and a bus terminal.
This is important, because lots of the employees live a long way away and come to work by train and bus. The company has a big car park (A): it has space for 500 vehicles.
There are two large buildings: the factory (L) and the office block (K).
Fletcher Industries produce their goods in the factory. The production department makes the products, so its offices (B, C and D) are situated here. There is also a canteen (E), toilets for male and female staff (F and G), and a small first-aid room (H). The area marked J is the packing area. Outside this is the loading bay: here the employees load finished goods onto trucks and unload raw materials from other companies.
The door to the office block leads into the reception area. On the first floor we find the offices of the marketing, sales and purchasing departments. The personnel department and accounts department have their offices on the second floor. The offices of the managing director, Miss Sarah Glover, and her secretary, Mrs Gloria James, are on the next floor. The board room, where the directors meet, is also here.

Wendungen und Begriffe

site	Firmengelände	*loading bay*	Ladeplatz
to be located	sich befinden	*raw materials*	Rohstoffe
vehicle	Fahrzeug	*to lead*	führen
factory	Fabrik	*floor*	Stock, Etage
first-aid	Erste Hilfe	*board room*	Konferenzraum
area	Fläche		

Übung 1

Unterstreichen Sie jeweils das Wort, das nicht in die Wortgruppe paßt.

1	2	3	4
truck	production	toilets	board room
car park	marketing	canteen	secretary
train	factory	floor	office
bus	accounts	first-aid room	loading bay

Übung 2

Vervollständigen Sie die Sätze mit Wörtern aus Übung 1.

1 When I feel hungry, I go to the __________________.

2 Our __________________ department advertises our goods.

3 Some of our staff travel to work by __________________.

4 If you do not feel well, go to the _________________________.

5 The directors meet in the _________________________.

6 Mr Miller's office is on the third ________________.

7 Our _________________________ department makes our goods.

8 We unload goods in the _________________________.

9 Visitors leave their cars in the __________________.

Übung 3

Suchen Sie mit Hilfe des Textes diese Ausdrücke und ihre Synonyme (bedeutungsähnliche Wörter) im Text.

1 located ________________________________

2 employees ________________________________

3 produce ________________________________

4 goods ________________________________

Übung 4

Suchen Sie die Antonyme (Wörter, die das Gegenteil bedeuten) im Text.

1 near ______________________________

2 large ______________________________

3 male ______________________________

4 load ______________________________

Übung 5

Vervollständigen Sie die Sätze mit passenden Ausdrücken aus dem Text.

1 My office is on the ground _______________ of the office block.

2 The company produces its goods in the _______________.

3 The _______________ can have lunch in the _______________.

4 Visitors leave their cars in the _______________.

5 We _______________ goods in the loading _______________.

6 The company makes finished goods from _______________ materials.

7 The two large _______________ are the office block and the factory.

8 The personnel _______________ has its _______________ on the second floor.

9 The directors _______________ in the _______________ room.

10 The _______________ director, Miss Glover, and her _______________ have offices on the third floor.

B The organization of the company

Diese Grafik zeigt den Aufbau der Firmenleitung von Fletcher Industries.

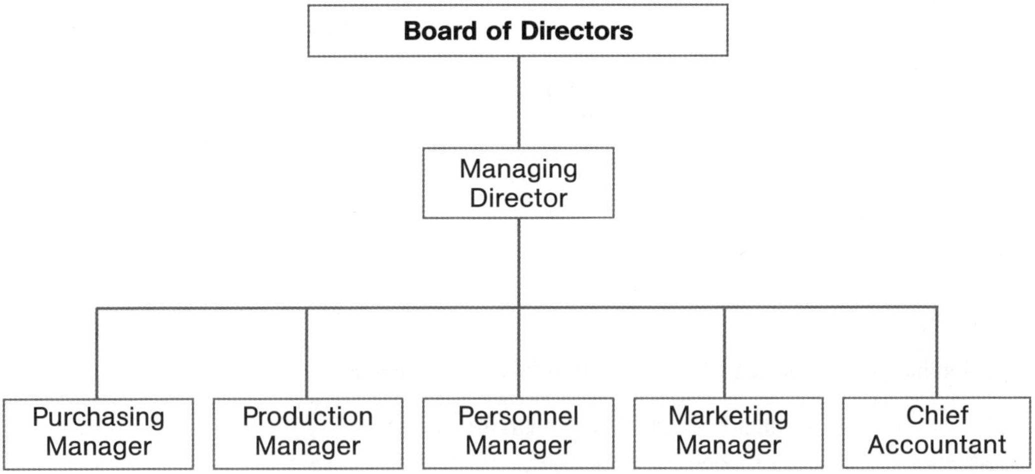

The Board of Directors has enormous responsibility. It makes the most important decisions about the company's activities. The directors appoint the managing director. This person is in charge of the management of the company. He or she appoints the managers, the people who run the departments in the company. And this person is responsible to the Board.

The purchasing manager is the head of the purchasing department.
This department buys the raw materials which the company needs. It also purchases furniture, equipment and supplies for the factory and the offices.

The production manager is responsible for the factory. He or she is also in charge of packaging and transport.

The personnel manager is in charge of the personnel department.
These people recruit staff and take care of them. They run the canteens and the first-aid room. Also, they look after employees who have problems at work.

The marketing manager heads the marketing and sales departments.
These departments find markets for goods. They advertise the company's goods, and sell as many of them as possible.

The chief accountant manages the accounts department.
Here the staff pay bills from suppliers. They also send invoices to customers. And they pay the salaries to the employees in the company.

Wendungen und Begriffe

Board of Directors	Firmenvorstand	*supplies*	Büromaterial, Bürobedarf
responsibility	Verantwortung	*to be responsible for*	für etw verantwortlich sein
decision	Entscheidung	*to recruit*	einstellen
to appoint	ernennen, berufen	*to take care of*	sich kümmern um
to run	leiten	*to look after*	sich kümmern um
department	Abteilung	*to head*	leiten, führen
to be responsible to	jdm gegenüber rechenschaftspflichtig/unterstellt sein	*to manage*	leiten
		invoice	Rechnung

Übung 6

Vervollständigen Sie diesen Absatz mit Hilfe folgender Wörter.

accountant • after • appoint • Board • buys • charge • customers • decisions • goods • head • invoices • responsible • runs • runs • sales

The ____________________ 1 of Directors is ____________________ 2 for making very important ____________________ 3. They ____________________ 4 the managing director, who ____________________ 5 the company. Each manager is in ____________________ 6 of a department. The chief ____________________ 7 pays the staff and sends ____________________ 8 to ____________________ 9. The purchasing manager ____________________ 10 goods from other companies. The personnel manager looks ____________________ 11 the employees. The production manager ____________________ 12 the production department, which makes the ____________________ 13. And the marketing manager is the ____________________ 14 of the marketing and ____________________ 15 departments.

Übung 7

Wer ist für folgendes verantwortlich?

1 Paying employees ____________________

2 Running the company ____________________

3 Making important decisions about what the company does ____________________

4 Looking after staff ____________________

5 Making goods ____________________

6 Selling products ____________________

7 Buying equipment ____________________

8 Advertising ____________________

Übung 8

Lesen Sie sich beide Texte noch einmal durch und übersetzen Sie diesen Abschnitt ins Englische.

Mein Büro liegt im Erdgeschoß des Fabrikgebäudes. Ich bin für die Produktionsabteilung verantwortlich und treffe Entscheidungen über die Waren, die die Firma herstellt. Ich bin dem Geschäftsführer gegenüber verantwortlich. Ich arbeite mit dem Marketing Manager zusammen, der für die Produkte, die wir produzieren, Werbung macht und sie verkauft. Ich arbeite auch mit dem Bilanzbuchhalter zusammen, der die Rechnungen für das Rohmaterial bezahlt.

3 Secretarial duties

A Receiving visitors

MRS JAMES Mr Schultz? I'm Gloria James, Miss Glover's secretary. Miss Glover has asked me to look after you for a few minutes. She's at a meeting at the moment, but she'll be free very shortly. She sends her apologies.

MR SCHULTZ That's quite all right.

MRS JAMES Can I get you some coffee?

MR SCHULTZ No, thank you. I had breakfast on the plane.

MRS JAMES How was your flight?

MR SCHULTZ Very comfortable, thank you.

MRS JAMES We've made a reservation for you at the Motorway Hotel. One of our drivers will take you there after your meeting this afternoon. It's very good, and close to London. And it's not far from here, so we find it very convenient. Would you like to leave your luggage in my office until later today?

MR SCHULTZ Yes, please. Do you know what my programme is?

MRS JAMES Yes. First you'll meet Miss Glover, our managing director. Then she'll introduce you to Mr Carling, the production manager, and Mr Dawson. Mr Dawson is responsible for sales in Britain and abroad. Mr Carling will show you the factory. After lunch Mr Dawson wants to discuss the German agency with you. By the way, are you free this evening?

MR SCHULTZ Yes, I am.

MRS JAMES That's good. Miss Glover would like to invite you to dinner in London. Ah, here she is. Miss Glover, I'd like you to meet Mr Schultz, our new German agent.

Wendungen und Begriffe

secretarial duty	Sekretariatsaufgabe	*flight*	Flug
to receive a visitor	einen (eine) Besucher(in) empfangen	*comfortable*	angenehm
shortly	in Kürze, bald	*close*	nahe, in der Nähe
to send your apologies	sich entschuldigen lassen	*convenient*	günstig
		luggage	Gepäck

Übung 1

Vervollständigen Sie die Tabelle.

Nouns	Verbs
apology	____________
flight	____________
reservation	____________
production	____________
sales	____________
manager	____________
____________	meet
____________	introduce
____________	discuss
____________	invite

Übung 2

Vervollständigen Sie diese Sätze mit Wörtern aus Übung 1.

1 We ____________ our goods in the factory.

2 I have just received an ____________ to lunch.

3 We must meet for a ____________ of these problems.

4 The managing director is at a ____________ with her agents.

5 I'll ____________ a table for dinner this evening.

6 Lufthansa and British Airways ____________ from Berlin to London.

7 I ____________ for arriving late. The traffic was very heavy.

8 Ann has agreed to ____________ the personnel department while Jan is off sick.

9 The company is not earning enough money: we must ____________ more goods to our customers!

10 I have a letter of ____________ to Mrs Gaunt. Do you know where she is?

Übung 3

Unterstreichen Sie jeweils das Wort, das nicht in die Wortgruppe paßt.

1	2	3
breakfast	secretary	comfortable
coffee	driver	good
lunch	reservation	convenient
dinner	managing director	later

Übung 4

Benutzen Sie Wörter aus Übung 3 im folgenden Absatz.

Before I go to work I have a good ____________________[1]. Then I go to the factory and there my ____________________[2] tells me who has telephoned. She also brings me a cup of ____________________[3].

I have ____________________[4] at 1.30 with my boss, the ____________________[5]. Sometimes we take guests to a restaurant for ____________________[6] in the evening. We always make a ____________________[7] first.

Übung 5

Ordnen Sie die Fragen und Antworten einander zu.

1	Did you have a good flight?	a	Good idea. Let's do that.
2	Are you free tomorrow?	b	Fine, thanks.
3	Can I get you a coffee?	c	Yes, it is actually.
4	Do you know what my programme is?	d	Yes, I am.
5	How about discussing this over lunch?	e	Yes, please, that'd be very nice.
6	Is this your first trip to Berlin?	f	I'm afraid not.

B Arranging meetings

Mr Dawson, der Verkaufsmanager, ist im Ausland auf Geschäftsreise. Er hat seiner Sekretärin, Miss Brown, ein Memo hinterlassen.

MEMORANDUM

To: *Linda*
From: *C. Dawson*
Date: *17 March 19..*
Subject: *SALES DEPARTMENT MEETING, 3 APRIL 19..*

Please send a memo to all our sales reps in Britain. We are holding the meeting here at Greenborough on 3 April at 10 a.m. in the conference room. There are four items on the agenda: minutes of the last meeting, sales figures for last year, our plans for the second half of this year, and AOB. Please do this ASAP. And please attend the meeting yourself – I would like you to take the minutes.

Thank you.

Charles Dawson

Wendungen und Begriffe

to arrange	arrangieren, vereinbaren
item	Punkt
agenda	Tagesordnung
minutes	Protokoll
to attend	teilnehmen

Übung 6

Dieses Memo enthält einige Abkürzungen. Welche stehen für diese Wendungen?

1 memorandum ______________________

2 representatives ______________________

3 in the morning ______________________

4 any other business ______________________

5 as soon as possible ______________________

Übung 7

Übersetzen Sie diese Wendungen.

1 any other business ____________________

2 as soon as possible ____________________

3 representatives ____________________

4 a.m. ____________________

Übung 8

Vervollständigen Sie Linda Browns Memo.

MEMORANDUM

To: All sales ____________[1]

From: ____________[2] manager

Date: 17 March 19..

Subject: SALES ____________[3] MEETING

Please ____________[4] this meeting ____________[5] Greenborough ____________[6] 3 April ____________[7] 10 a.m. in the ____________[8] room.

There are four ____________[9] on the ____________[10]:

1 ____________[11]

2 ____________[12]

3 ____________[13]

4 ____________[14]

Thank you.

Linda Brown

____________[15] to sales manager

Übung 9

Ordnen Sie die Satzhälften einander zu.

1	Is there any	a	on business.
2	There are six items	b	takes the minutes.
3	All the representatives	c	as soon as possible.
4	He is in Germany	d	will attend the meeting.
5	A secretary	e	on the agenda.
6	Please send the memo	f	other business?

Übung 10

Übersetzen Sie die Sätze von Übung 9.

1 ______________________________

2 ______________________________

3 ______________________________

4 ______________________________

5 ______________________________

6 ______________________________

Übung 11

Unterstreichen Sie jeweils das Wort, das nicht in die Wortgruppe paßt.

1	2	3	4
memo	sales rep	item	hold
minutes	secretary	agenda	plan
agenda	sales manager	minutes	write
sales figures	Board of Directors	any other business	attend
telephone call	marketing manager	conference room	arrange

4 Telephoning

A Long distance calls

INTERNATIONAL DIALLING

International Direct Dialling – IDD – is the quick, easy way to telephone abroad. Look up the code in the telephone book. If it is not shown, ask the international operator for it. What could be easier?
International Direct Dialling enables you to dial over 170 countries around the world. Already over 98% of international calls made from the UK are dialled direct, and more countries are added each year.

Operator Calls

If you can't dial direct, then make the call through the international operator on 155. Similarly, if you require a special service such as a collect (transfer charge) or personal call, the international operator can tell you if it is available in the country you want to call.

This is how to use it

International Direct Dialling is based on a standard system comprising four elements:

FIRST dial the international code. From the UK this is always 00.

THEN dial the country code. These are listed in the telephone book.

NEXT dial the area code.

THEN dial the customer's number you want.

Wendungen und Begriffe

code	Vorwahl	*similarly*	genauso
operator	Vermittlung	*to require*	benötigen, wünschen
to enable	ermöglichen	*collect call (AE)*	R-Gespräch
to dial	anwählen	*available*	verfügbar
to add	hinzufügen, hinzukommen	*to comprise*	bestehen aus

Übung 1

Vervollständigen Sie die Sätze mit passenden Wörtern aus dem Text.

1 IDD stands for International Direct ________________.

2 The international ________________ from Britain is 00.

3 If you want to call a number in Hamburg, first you dial the ________________ ________________ for Germany.

4 Then you need the ________________ ________________ for Hamburg.

5 Finally, you dial the ________________ number.

6 We cannot call some countries direct, so we go through the ________________ ________________.

7 A collect call is sometimes called a ________________ ________________ call.

8 If you want to speak to a particular person, you can make a ________________ call.

9 The international operator can give us information about special ________________________________.

Übung 2

Finden Sie die Antonyme im Text.

1 slow ________________________________

2 difficult ________________________________

3 in this country ________________________________

4 fewer ________________________________

5 can't ________________________________

Übung 3

Ordnen Sie die Satzhälften einander zu.

1 We must look up	a the international code.
2 Special services	b in the telephone book.
3 IDD lets us telephone	c under country entries.
4 First we dial	d almost 200 countries.
5 Country codes are listed	e are things like personal calls or collect calls.
6 We find area codes	f the right area code.

B Taking messages

TELEPHONIST	Fletcher Industries, good afternoon.
CALLER	May I speak to Mr Dawson, please?
TELEPHONIST	I'm afraid he's at a meeting at the moment. Can I take a message?
CALLER	This is Antje Ravens, the managing director of Müller GmbH.
TELEPHONIST	I'm sorry, but I don't speak Spanish. Would you spell that, please?
CALLER	Certainly. And it's German. My name is Antje Ravens. First name capital A, then small n, t, j, e. Last name capital R, then small a, v, e, n, s. The name of my company is spelled with a capital M, small u, e, double l, e, r.
TELEPHONIST	Thank you. And your message, please?
CALLER	Please ask Mr Dawson to call me as soon as possible. It's urgent.
TELEPHONIST	Of course. I'll tell his secretary when she gets back from lunch. Thank you for calling.
CALLER	Thank you. Goodbye.

Wendungen und Begriffe

to take a message	eine Nachricht übermitteln
to spell	buchstabieren
capital	Großbuchstabe
urgent	dringend

Übung 4

Übersetzen Sie ins Deutsche.

1 May I speak to …? ______________________________

2 I'm afraid … ______________________________

3 Can I take a message? ______________________________

4 I'm sorry, … ______________________________

5 Would you spell that, please? ______________________________

6 Certainly. ______________________________

7 First name ______________________________

8 Capital "a" ______________________________

9 Last name ______________________________

10 Small "e" ______________________________

11 It's urgent. ______________________________

12 Thank you for calling. ______________________________

Übung 5

Buchstabieren Sie diese Namen. Benutzen Sie jeweils die Begriffe *first name, last name, capital* und *small.*

1 Simon Yeats
2 William Younger
3 Frances Jacobs
4 Christine House
5 Paul Kingston
6 David Templeton
7 Georgina Quaver
8 Victor Hamilton

Da es im englischen Alphabet kein ä, ö, ü und ß gibt, sollten Sie sie mit ae, oe, ue und ss angeben. Üben Sie dies anhand folgender Namen:

9 Gerhardt Pfühl
10 Bärbel Walther
11 Albrecht Götz
12 Jürgen Süßkind
13 Maria Groß

Übung 6

Schreiben Sie einen Dialog zwischen Uta Hübner, Götz Metall KG, Berlin und einer Telefonistin bei Fletcher Industries. Benutzen Sie einige von den vorher verwendeten Ausdrücken und Ihre eigenen. Es ist 10.30 Uhr.

TELEPHONIST (Answers the telephone.)

____ 1

UTA HÜBNER (Asks to speak to Miss Glover.)

May ____ 2

TELEPHONIST (Explains that unfortunately, Miss Glover is in Birmingham on business. Offers to take a message.)

I'm ________ 3 but Miss ______________________________ 4

Birmingham. Can ________ 5 take ______________________________ 6?

UTA HÜBNER (Introduces herself.)

____ 7

TELEPHONIST (Asks caller to spell her name.)

____ 8

UTA HÜBNER (Spells her name.)

Certainly. ____ 9

TELEPHONIST (Thanks caller. Asks what the message is.)

____ 10

UTA HÜBNER (Tells telephonist that it is not urgent. She will call again next week.)

____

____ 11

TELEPHONIST (Thanks caller for calling.)

____ 12

Travelling 5

A Making reservations

Miss Sarah Glover, Geschäftsführerin bei Fletcher Industries, fährt nach Deutschland. Ihre Sekretärin, Mrs Gloria James, bereitet die Reise für sie vor.

Mr Long	Global Travel, good morning.
Mrs James	Morning. I'd like to book a return flight, London – Berlin, please.
Mr Long	Yes, of course. What's the departure date?
Mrs James	Monday 12 May. I'd like an early morning flight if possible.
Mr Long	There are seats available on Lufthansa LH 2524, leaving London Heathrow at 9 a.m. And British Airways have a flight an hour earlier.
Mrs James	The Lufthansa flight, please. One person, business class.
Mr Long	I'm sorry. Did you say economy class?
Mrs James	No, business. The passenger's name is Miss Sarah Glover. That's G-L-O-V-E-R.
Mr Long	And when will Miss Glover be leaving Berlin?
Mrs James	On a late afternoon flight on Friday 16 May.
Mr Long	I can reserve her a business class seat on BA 986, departing at 6 p.m. Is that suitable?
Mrs James	Yes, that's fine, thank you. And Miss Glover will need a car and a room at a first-class hotel near the Kurfürstendamm from 12 to 15 May inclusive. Can you arrange that as well?
Mr Long	Certainly. I'll fax the Hilton this afternoon and make a reservation. It's a five-star hotel. Would Miss Glover rather have a large car or a small one? And does she want a driver?
Mrs James	A small one will be fine and without a driver, please.
Mr Long	I'll call you later this afternoon to confirm the bookings. Or would you prefer me to send a fax?
Mrs James	A fax, please. The number is ...

Wendungen und Begriffe

return flight	Rückflug	*rather*	lieber
departure	Abflug	*to confirm*	bestätigen
seat	Platz	*booking*	Buchung
suitable	passend		

Übung 1

Vervollständigen Sie die Tabelle mit den passenden Substantiven und Verben. Einige finden Sie im Dialog auf Seite 27.

Nouns	Verbs
fax	____________
reservation	____________
departure	____________
driver	____________
____________	confirm
____________	arrange
____________	call
____________	book

Übung 2

Vervollständigen Sie die Sätze mit Ausdrücken aus dem Dialog.

1 Flying ____________ ____________ is less expensive than flying business class.

2 A single ticket will take you from London to Berlin. If you want to fly from London to Berlin and back to London, you need a ____________ ticket.

3 If you want to stay at a hotel, you should make a ____________, which means the same as a booking.

4 I want to spend most of the day in Berlin, so please book me a seat on a ____________ ____________ ____________ back to London.

5 There are no ____________ ____________ on the British Airways flight, but I can book you on Lufthansa.

Übung 3

Übersetzen Sie ins Deutsche.

1 de luxe ______________________

2 economy class ______________________

3 dinner ______________________

4 late night ______________________

5 lunch ______________________

Übung 4

Ordnen Sie die folgenden Wörter der richtigen Wortgruppe zu.

breakfast • late afternoon • five-star • early morning • business class • economy class • first class • luxury • dinner • lunch • late night

Hotel classifications	Meals
______________________	______________________
______________________	______________________
______________________	______________________
______________________	______________________
______________________	______________________

Timings of airline flights	Types of airline seat
______________________	______________________
______________________	______________________
______________________	______________________
______________________	______________________
______________________	______________________

B Arriving at a foreign airport

Dieses Informationsblatt wird an Reisende ausgegeben, die nach Kwonga, einem kleinen, eher unbekannten Land in Asien fahren. Es enthält wichtige Informationen über Einreisebestimmungen.

DEMOCRATIC REPUBLIC OF KWONGA

WELCOME TO MAI LU AIRPORT

When your aircraft lands, go directly to the baggage reclaim area and collect your luggage. Proceed without delay to Airport Security. Then go immediately to Immigration and show your passport, visa and landing card. The immigration official will stamp your passport, check your visa and keep half of your landing card. You must retain all your travel documents during your stay in the Democratic Republic of Kwonga. You must return your visa and the other half of your landing card when you leave the Republic. Remember: your stay is restricted to fifteen days.

Then proceed to Customs. Customs officials will ask you to open suitcases, bags, briefcases and other items of luggage. They will also ask you how much money you have, and in which currencies. It is strictly forbidden to import or export Kwongan guas, but you may import other currencies, like American dollars, Swiss francs and German marks, in unlimited amounts.

The following are prohibited: dangerous drugs, political and religious literature, weapons, and decadent magazines. You may import one litre of wine and/or spirits and as much beer as you like. There is a limit of 200 cigarettes per passenger. These are duty-free.

The airport has a bureau de change, a restaurant (foreign currency only) and a taxi rank. Other airport facilities include restrooms and a bar where you can enjoy typical Kwongan drinks.

Please leave the airport by the door marked “Exit” and take a taxi to your hotel.

HAVE A PLEASANT STAY IN KWONGA

Wendungen und Begriffe

baggage reclaim area	Gepäckausgabe	*unlimited*	unbegrenzt
without delay	unverzüglich	*amount*	Höhe, Menge
to retain	behalten	*decadent*	dekadent
to return	zurückgeben	*foreign*	ausländisch
restricted	beschränkt, begrenzt	*taxi rank*	Taxistand
to proceed	begeben	*facilities*	Einrichtung
currency	Währung	*restrooms (AE)*	Toiletten

Übung 5

Ordnen Sie diese Begriffe verschiedenen Oberbegriffen zu.

visa • mark • restrooms • spirits • dollar • bag • bar • taxi rank • landing card • briefcase • wine • restaurant • suitcase • passport • franc • beer • bureau de change

Luggage: ______________________________

Documents: ______________________________

Drinks: ______________________________

Currencies: ______________________________

Airport facilities: ______________________________

Übung 6

Suchen Sie für diese Sätze jeweils den richtigen Ausdruck im Text.

1 A person who checks your travel documents ____________________

2 People who examine your luggage ____________________

3 Heroin and cocaine ____________________

4 Guns and knives ____________________

5 *Der Spiegel, Time* and *Playboy* ____________________

6 Whisky and brandy ____________________

7 Tax which you pay on imported goods ____________________

Übung 7

Suchen Sie Synonyme für diese Wörter im Text. Sie können auch Ihr Wörterbuch zu Hilfe nehmen.

1 immediately (adverb) ______________________

2 keep (verb) ______________________

3 give back (verb) ______________________

4 articles (noun) ______________________

5 unrestricted (adj) ______________________

6 forbidden (adj) ______________________

7 tax-free (adj) ______________________

Übung 8

Vervollständigen Sie diese kurze Anweisung mit Wörtern und Ausdrücken aus dem Text.

WELCOME TO HEATHROW ______________[1], LONDON.

When you have shown your ______________[2] at ______________[3], please collect your ______________[4] at the ______________ ______________[5] area. Then go directly to Customs, where you must pay ______________[6] on goods which are not ______________[7]. You may import pounds sterling and ______________[8] currencies in unlimited ______________[9].

WE HOPE YOU HAVE A PLEASANT STAY IN BRITAIN.

Buying 6

A An enquiry

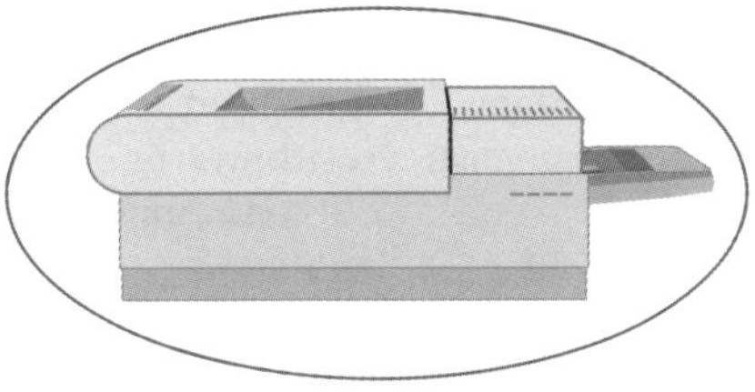

MR NORMAN Hello, Mrs Bridges. I'd like to ask you a few questions about your new laser printer. We've had a look at it, and we'd like to place an order. But we need some information first.

MRS BRIDGES Of course, Mr Norman. It's just come onto the market, and we've had a lot of enquiries. It's very popular. Some wholesalers are already ordering large numbers. Now, what information can I give you?

MR NORMAN First, what about wholesale prices? And discounts?

MRS BRIDGES The unit price is $275. We can grant you a 10% discount on orders worth $27,500 or more. And we can allow larger discounts for bigger orders. Our prices are very competitive. Our customers are satisfied with the high quality, and they're very pleased with the price.

MR NORMAN Do you have large stocks? We need 200 soon.

MRS BRIDGES We can supply you within three weeks. But the printers are in great demand. I advise you to order very soon.

MR NORMAN What are your terms of payment?

MRS BRIDGES For new customers, we ask for cash with the order. But you've bought equipment from us in the past, haven't you?

MR NORMAN Yes, we've been doing business with you for a year or so.

MRS BRIDGES Then our conditions will be cash within 30 days. We can discuss other terms later.

MR NORMAN Fine. Well, as I said we need the printers urgently – by the end of next week. Is that possible?

MRS BRIDGES Yes, we can send them by special delivery, but you will have to pay a small extra charge. When can we expect your order?

MR NORMAN I'll send it to you by fax this morning.

MRS BRIDGES Thank you, Mr Norman. Goodbye for now.

Wendungen und Begriffe

enquiry	Anfrage	*stock*	Bestand
to place an order	eine Bestellung bei jdm aufgeben, jdm einen Auftrag geben	*to supply*	liefern, versorgen
wholesaler	Großhändler(in)	*in great demand*	sehr gefragt sein
unit price	Einheitspreis	*to advise*	empfehlen
to grant	gewähren	*terms of payment*	Zahlungsbedingungen
competitive	wettbewerbs-, konkurrenzfähig	*equipment*	Geräte
satisfied	zufrieden	*urgently*	dringend
		special delivery	Eilzustellung
		extra charge	Zuschlag

Übung 1

Suchen Sie im Dialog die Antonyme.

1 less ________________

2 smaller ________________

3 old ________________

4 in the future ________________

5 sooner ________________

6 the beginning of ________________

Übung 2

Bilden Sie Antonyme, indem Sie die richtigen Vorsilben, *im-*, *dis-* oder *un-*, hinzufügen.

1 popular ________________

2 satisfied ________________

3 possible ________________

4 like ________________

5 pleased ________________

Übung 3

Vervollständigen Sie die Tabelle mit den passenden Verben und Substantiven.

Nouns	Verbs	Nouns	Verbs
information	______________	______________	allow
enquiry	______________	______________	need
guarantee	______________	______________	offer
delivery	______________	______________	advise
stocks	______________	______________	discuss

Übung 4

Vervollständigen Sie diese Sätze mit Wörtern aus Übung 3. Ein Wort wurde dreimal benutzt.

1 A I would like to ______________ about a new fax machine. Can you help me?

B Yes, we have a lot of ______________ on our new model, the FX 90. I'll send it to you and then after you have had a look, we can ______________ details over the phone.

2 I'm afraid we cannot ______________ to your office before January because our ______________ are very low at the moment.

3 Do your new fax machines have a 12-month ______________?

4 If you ______________ any after-sales ______________, please ring me on 0171 943 1223.

5 We can ______________ you a discount of 10%.

6 You ______________ a CX 200? I'm sorry, I can't help you there. It's an old model and I'm afraid we don't ______________ it any more.

7 Don't buy now. I ______________ you to wait until the sales after Christmas.

8 No Bob, I don't want any more ______________ on this subject. The plain paper fax is simply too expensive. We really don't ______________ one and so I'm not going to buy one.

Übung 5

Vervollständigen Sie die Sätze mit den Wörtern aus Übung 3.

1 There is a great ______________ for computers in business.

2 We ______________ that our products are in good condition.

3 The company ______________ large numbers of articles in its warehouse.

4 The customer is ______________ about the new model.

5 He gave us some ______________ about where to buy laser printers.

6 My father used to give me an ______________ of DM 5 a week.

7 We must ______________ these problems very soon.

8 Their ______________ is very good, and we are going to accept it.

9 They always ______________ goods by air.

10 The supplier will ______________ us about prices and delivery dates.

Übung 6

Übersetzen Sie diesen Absatz ins Englische.

Unsere Preise sind sehr konkurrenzbewußt und wir geben großen Rabatt. Die Qualität der Produkte ist hoch und unsere Kunden sind sehr zufrieden. Die Waren werden am Ende der Woche per Eilzustellung geliefert.

____

____

____

____

____

____

B Choosing where to buy

What does the customer need?

How does he/she want to pay?

Where can he/she get what he/she wants?

How much can he/she afford to pay?

What quality does he/she want?

When does he/she need the goods?

Customers often have to choose between several suppliers. Some manufacturers and dealers sell high-quality products, and these are often more expensive. Not everyone can afford a large BMW or Mercedes-Benz, so they look for a less expensive car. Then they have to discuss delivery times and terms of payment.

Dealer A may have a suitable car in stock, but dealer B may ask his customer to wait for a few weeks. But dealer A might want cash, and dealer B might offer credit. After-sales service is also important. Shop Y is offering a Kimsung computer at DM 500, and shop Z has the same article on special offer for DM 400. But shopkeeper Y provides a two-year guarantee, and shopkeeper Z guarantees the product for one year only.

Consumers think about terms of payment, too. Shop Y allows customers to buy on hire purchase terms: this means they pay a deposit of DM 50, and the balance over a year. But shop B sells on cash terms: the customer has to pay the whole price before he takes the merchandise out of the shop.

Consumers ought to be price-conscious and quality-conscious. They should look around before deciding where to purchase. If, for example, you want a new camera, go to a number of different shops and ask about discounts, credit and other matters. The more time you spend, the more money you can save.

Wendungen und Begriffe

dealer	Händler(in)	*on special offer*	im/als Sonderangebot
to afford	sich leisten	*on hire purchase terms*	auf Raten
to have sth in stock	etw vorrätig haben, etw am Lager haben	*merchandise*	Ware
		price-conscious	preisbewußt

Übung 7

Finden Sie die Entsprechung zu diesen *kursiv* gedruckten Ausdrücken im Text.

1 I *have enough money for* a new house.

____

2 Some cars *cost more* than others.

____

3 We are worried about *when the goods will be sent.*

____

4 Some suppliers ask customers to pay *money* at once.

____

5 If you are lucky, you can find goods *at especially low prices.*

____

6 I am paying for my computer *over a year.*

____

7 I will pay half the price now, and the *rest* over six months.

____

8 We normally pay for *goods* in the shop.

____

9 Most buyers *think a lot about prices and quality.*

____

10 When you *buy* large quantities, you will receive a discount.

____

Übung 8

Welches Wort paßt nicht in die Wortgruppe?

1	2	3	4
supplier	manufacturers	cash	buy
dealer	goods	credit	purchase
customer	merchandise	hire purchase	save
shopkeeper	products	after-sales service	pay for

Übung 9

Bilden Sie Sätze mit den vier aussortierten Wörtern aus Übung 8.

1 ______________________________

2 ______________________________

3 ______________________________

4 ______________________________

Übung 10

Ordnen Sie die Satzhälften einander zu.

1	I cannot afford	a	than a small one.
2	Some suppliers ask for cash,	b	for a year.
3	We guarantee the article	c	be price-conscious.
4	They are talking about terms	d	between different suppliers.
5	A large house is more expensive	e	in stock.
6	We are offering this model	f	you can save money.
7	All customers should	g	to pay a lot of money.
8	Buyers can choose	h	of payment.
9	We have several models	i	at DM 1,000.
10	If you shop carefully,	j	but others allow credit.

7 Selling

A A sale

Sehen Sie sich die Anzeige und den nachfolgenden Dialog an.

SAKSDALE'S DEPARTMENT STORE

will hold its annual

SALE

from 1 to 10 January.

We are offering thousands of articles at unbelievably low prices.
Reductions of 50% on all clothing.
Save hundreds of dollars on furniture.
Buy your new stereo system at a huge discount.
All our curtains and carpets are on sale at 75 % of normal prices.

CLERK Can I help you?

CUSTOMER I'd like to buy a good cassette recorder.

CLERK Then I can recommend this one. The original price was $250.00, but the sale price is half of that: $125.00. It's a real bargain.

CUSTOMER Oh, I don't want to spend as much as that. Do you have anything similar at a lower price?

CLERK Yes, but the quality isn't the same. This one is made in Germany. The materials and workmanship are first class. It has a two-year guarantee, too.

CUSTOMER I see. Can I pay a deposit now, and the rest next month?

CLERK I'm sorry, but we can't allow credit during the sale. All goods are sold for cash only.

CUSTOMER All right, I'll pay cash. Will you deliver it to my house, please?

CLERK I'm afraid not. Our terms for all purchases are cash and carry until the sale ends.

CUSTOMER Then I'll take it with me.

CLERK Thank you. Would you mind going to the cash desk where you can pay and collect your cassette recorder?

CUSTOMER Sure. Thank you.

Wendungen und Begriffe

sale	Verkauf	*workmanship*	Arbeitsqualität
to recommend	empfehlen	*deposit*	Anzahlung
bargain	Sonderangebot, wirklich günstig	*to allow credit*	Kredit geben
		to deliver	liefern
similar	ähnlich	*cash and carry*	Abholpreis

Übung 1

Vervollständigen Sie die Sätze.

save • deposit • buy • goods • price • cash • discount • sale • deliver • department store

1 Customers go to shops to ______________ things they need.

2 If you do not spend your money, you can ______________ it.

3 The ________________________ of this article is $10.00.

4 You will find hundreds of different ______________ at a supermarket.

5 The store is offering big reductions at its ______________.

6 We do not allow credit – our customers pay ______________.

7 If you want to buy furniture, curtains, radios and other goods, go to a ________________________.

8 Some stores ________________________ goods to their customers' homes.

9 If you buy three of these articles, we can offer you a ________________________.

10 You can pay a ______________ of 20% now, and the rest later.

Übung 2

Übersetzen Sie ins Englische.

Bei unserem jährlichen Schlußverkauf bieten wir unseren Kunden eine große Auswahl zu unglaublich günstigen Preisen. Sie können alles zu Sonderangebotspreisen bekommen: Wir bieten Ihnen einen großen Rabatt. Und wir liefern alles frei Haus.

Übung 3

Vervollständigen Sie die Sätze mit dem passenden Wort.

1. If you want a real (bargain/offer) come to our sale!
2. We (save/deliver) free of charge.
3. We have thousands of (reductions/articles) on sale.
4. You can (save/credit) hundreds of dollars at our sale.
5. Our terms are (on sale/cash and carry).
6. You pay a small (deposit/offer) when you buy these goods.

B Wholesalers and retailers

Hello, everyone. My name's Bill Davis, and I'm a fruit wholesaler. I buy fruit in large quantities from producers, and sell it in smaller quantities to retailers.

My suppliers are orange growers in Morocco and Spain. My customers are supermarkets, chain stores, department stores and small shopkeepers in the south of England. My customers then sell the fruit to you, the consumers.

Basically it works like this: I buy a kilo of oranges for 25 pence, and I have to sell it for about 50 pence. This is because I have to cover my costs and, of course, make a profit. Nobody wants to make a loss! Also, a shop which buys a kilo from me for 50 pence will sell it to you for about a pound.

Most of the oranges I buy go to the big supermarkets. The chain stores like Marks and Spencers and Woolworths are my next biggest customers. These shops sell a wider range of products than the supermarkets. Besides foodstuffs, they deal in clothing, furniture, toys and a number of other products.

Department stores buy quite a lot of oranges from me, but food is not one of their biggest lines. They specialize in other things, such as furniture, stereo systems and so on.

Finally, there are the small greengrocers. These shops are no longer very important – the big supermarkets and chain stores are slowly replacing them.

Wendungen und Begriffe

retailer	Einzelhändler(in)	*range*	Sortiment
grower	Züchter(in)	*foodstuffs*	Nahrungsmittel
to cover your costs	die Kosten decken	*to deal in*	handeln mit
loss	Verlust	*line*	Posten, Warensortiment
wider	breiter, umfangreicher	*to replace*	ersetzen

Übung 4

Finden Sie die entsprechenden Ausdrücke zu diesen Sätzen im Text.

1 People or organizations that produce oranges.

____

2 A person or organization that buys from a producer and sells to shops.

____

3 People or organizations that buy from wholesalers.

____

4 Large shops which sell food.

____

5 People who buy goods from shops.

____

6 Usually small shops which sell only fruit and vegetables.

____

7 Large shops that sell products like chairs, tables, washing machines and VCRs.

____

8 To sell goods for more than you pay for them.

____

Übung 5

Ordnen Sie diese Begriffe in vier Gruppen ein.

consumers • chain stores • wholesalers • cover costs • supermarkets • producers • make a loss • products • department stores • make a profit • retailers • greengrocers • foodstuffs • sell for 25p

Group 1

____
____
____
____

Group 2

____
____
____
____

Group 3

____
____
____
____

Group 4

____
____
____
____

Übung 6

Vervollständigen Sie die Tabelle, indem Sie die fehlenden Substantive einfügen.

Verbs	Nouns
consume	______________
retail	______________
produce	______________
grow	______________
sell	______________
buy	______________

Banking and payments 8

A Banks and their services

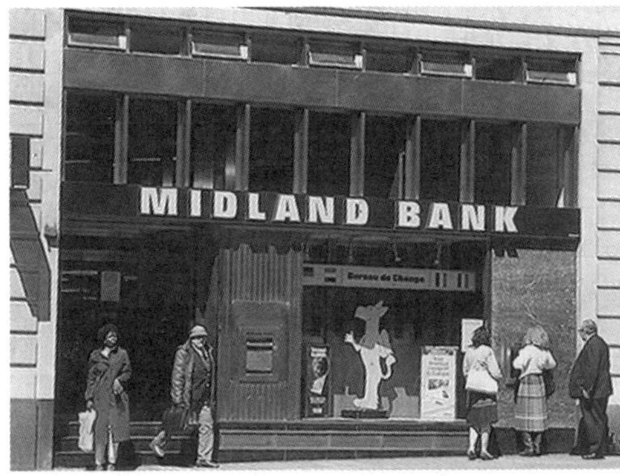

In diesem Text erfahren Sie etwas über die Dienste, die Banken ihren Kunden anbieten.

Most people keep their money in the bank, not at home. They do this because their money is safer, because it earns interest and because banks offer their customers useful services.

There are two main types of bank account: current accounts and savings accounts. A customer's employer pays his salary into a current account every month. We can withdraw money from a current account by writing out a cheque or by using a cash card. We can also pay bills by making out cheques to our creditors.

Some banks send a statement every month. The statement lists the deposits and withdrawals. The final figure on the statement is the balance: how much money we have in our account at the end of the month.

We use a savings account in order to save money for a holiday, a car or our old age. We can arrange for the bank to transfer a sum of money from our current account to our savings account every month. And our money earns interest in a savings account.

Banks also issue customers with cash cards. We can use a cash card to withdraw money from a cash dispenser, and to pay for goods and services.

Sometimes we need to borrow money. A bank usually grants loans or overdrafts to good customers, but normally it asks for security when it lends money.

Wendungen und Begriffe

to earn interest	Zinsen bringen	*balance*	Kontostand
to withdraw	abheben	*to issue*	ausstellen
bill	Rechnung	*cash dispenser*	Geldautomat
creditor	Gläubiger(in)	*to grant a loan*	ein Darlehen gewähren
statement	Kontoauszug		
deposit	Einzahlung	*overdraft*	Kontoüberziehung
withdrawal	Auszahlung	*security*	Sicherheit

Übung 1

Entscheiden Sie sich für den passenden (*kursiv* geschriebenen) Ausdruck.

1 If we keep our money in the bank, it is *safe/useful.*
2 We can pay bills by writing out *statements/cheques.*
3 If we have a savings account, we earn *deposits/interest* on our money.
4 If we are going abroad, we need foreign *salary/currency.*
5 Banks *transfer/deposit* money from one account to another.
6 You can *deposit/withdraw* money in your account at any time.
7 Banks send customers a *statement/figure* every month.
8 Banks ask for *balances/security* before they grant loans.

Übung 2

Im letzten Absatz des Textes finden Sie die Verben *to borrow* und *to lend.* Sehen Sie sich diese Beispiele an.

Customers *borrow* money from banks.
Banks *lend* money to customers.

Setzen sie nun das entsprechende Verb ein.

1 I haven't got any money, but I'll try to ________________ some from my father.
2 My girlfriend has promised to ________________ me $100, but I'll have to pay her back next month.
3 The World Bank is going to ________________ five million dollars to countries in Africa.
4 I'm going to a party this evening. May I ________________ a tie from you?
5 I never ________________ money, not even to my best friends.
6 My car has broken down, so I'll have to ________________ my sister's.
7 Can you ________________ me $50 until tomorrow, please?
8 Would you mind if I ________________ this book? I'll return it to you next week, I promise.

Übung 3

Ordnen Sie diese Begriffe den folgenden drei Oberbegriffen zu.

salary • cash • savings • cheque • cash card • statement • loan • deposits • currency • withdrawals • bills

Money	Documents	Banking services
________	________	________
________	________	________
________	________	________
________	________	________
________	________	________
________	________	________
________	________	________

Übung 4

Vervollständigen Sie die Tabelle.

Nouns	Verbs
advice	________
loan	________
service	________
savings	________
employer	________
________	earn
________	pay
________	deposit
________	withdraw
________	transfer

B Paying for goods and services

Jennifer Morely, Leiterin der Buchhaltung von Fletcher Industries, informiert den Interviewer über die Zahlungsbedingungen ihrer Firma.

INTERVIEWER Do you grant credit to all your customers?

MRS MORELY Only to customers that have done business with us for over a year. We allow them quarterly terms. That means we send them an invoice with each order, and a statement every three months. They don't pay us anything until they receive their statement every quarter.

INTERVIEWER What's the difference between an invoice and a statement?

MRS MORELY I'll show you an invoice. It shows details of what we sent to a customer on a certain date. It lists the number of goods, the unit price, transport and insurance costs, and the total price.
Now this, on the other hand, is a statement. It shows all the transactions – the credits and debits – for three months. The final figure is the balance.

News International Associated Services Ltd.
Accounting Centre, P. O. Box 8, Peterborough PE1 1SF
Tel: (01733) 555333

CORNELSEN & OXFORD
UNIVERSITY PRESS
JOHANNISBERGER STR. 74
14197 BERLIN
GERMANY

PERIOD END	31/03/96	ACCOUNT CONTACT	KATIE ROE
ACCOUNT NUMBER	F/902451	PAGE NUMBER	1/1

		TRANSACTION								
Your Reference	Sales Ref	Date	Number	Type	Status	Cross Ref	Due Date Amount	Original Amount	Outstanding	Balance
		02/01/96	9410				02/02/96		65.00	65.00
		24/01/96	9531				24/02/96		32.00	32.00
		08/02/96	9593				08/03/96		50.00	50.00
		15/03/96	9700				15/04/96		13.00	13.00
		25/03/96	9981				25/04/96		97.00	97.00

STATEMENT

THE J. ALLAN CASH PHOTOLIBRARY
J. Allan Cash Ltd. 74 South Ealing Road, London, W5 5QB. Tel: 0181-840 4141

Invoice

Dr Blanca-Maria Rudhart
Cornelsen & Oxford University Press
Johannisberger Str. 74
14197 Berlin
GERMANY

Invoice No. 2591
Our Ref. 7661/INV 1217
Your Ref.
Miss Sophie & Other Lives
Tax Point 15/12/95

Repro fees on 4 b/w subjects		
246/280 used up to 5000 sq mm	32	00
S6447, 327/213, used up to 10,000 sq mm	105	75

INTERVIEWER And how do your other customers pay?

MRS MORELY We ask them to pay cash when they order. But some of them pay by cheque, of course.

INTERVIEWER	And how do you pay your staff and your own suppliers? And other people?
MRS MORELY	We pay salaries to all our employees. That means we pay them monthly. Some years ago we used to pay our factory staff wages – we paid them every week. Nowadays we transfer salaries to our employees' bank accounts on the last day of each month. It's much easier than writing out cheques or putting cash in pay packets. We often have to pay fees to lawyers and consultants. When they send us their invoices, we send them cheques. Our suppliers grant us credit, and we pay them quarterly.
INTERVIEWER	Thank you, Mrs Morely.

Wendungen und Begriffe

to grant credit	Kredit geben/gewähren	*transaction*	Abschluß, Transaktion
quarterly terms	vierteljährliche Frist	*wage*	Lohn
invoice	Rechnung	*pay packet*	Lohntüte
statement	Auszug	*fee*	Gebühr, Honorar
insurance	Versicherung		

Übung 5

Ordnen Sie den zehn Definitionen die passenden Ausdrücke zu, die im Interview verwendet wurden.

1 Every three months. ______________________

2 A document which shows the price of an order. ______________________

3 A document showing a customer how much he owes for goods supplied over 3 months. ______________________

4 What one article costs. ______________________

5 What a company pays to insure goods. ______________________

6 The difference between what a customer owes and what he has paid. ______________________

7 Banknotes and coins. ______________________

8 Monthly payments for employees. ______________________

9 Weekly payments for employees. ______________________

10 Payments made to doctors, lawyers, etc. ______________________

Übung 6

Streichen Sie den Begriff, der nicht in die jeweilige Wortgruppe paßt.

1	2	3	4
employees	invoice	wages	insurance costs
customers	statement	credit	fees
suppliers	staff	salaries	unit price
transactions	cheque	cash	transport costs

Übung 7

Wählen Sie je einen Oberbegriff für die vier Wortgruppen aus Übung 6.

documents • money • people in business • expenses • letters • prices • banking • employers

1 ______________________________

2 ______________________________

3 ______________________________

4 ______________________________

Übung 8

Ordnen Sie die Satzhälften einander zu.

1 Statements are sent	a credits and debits.
2 Most customers pay	b monthly.
3 We grant	c is the balance.
4 An invoice lists	d by cheque.
5 Salaries are paid	e the goods and prices.
6 The final figure on a statement	f credit to some customers.
7 Invoices are sent	g every three months.
8 Transactions are	h with orders.

Applications and interviews 9

A Applying for a job

MADDISON INDUSTRIES PLC

235 GRANTONE STREET
MANCHESTER MA21 U87

12 August 199.

Miss Julia Grayson
12 Jackson Road
MANCHESTER
MA23 P14

Dear Miss Grayson

Thank you for applying for the post of secretary to our purchasing manager. Your letter of application and your curriculum vitae are very impressive. We would like to invite you to attend an interview here on Monday 19 August at 10 a.m. You will then meet Mr Ashcroft, our purchasing manager, and myself.
Please telephone my secretary to confirm the appointment, or, if the time is not convenient for you, to make a new one.
We look forward to meeting you soon.

Yours sincerely
MADDISON INDUSTRIES PLC

Andrea Collins
Andrea Collins
Personnel Manager

Wendungen und Begriffe

impressive	beeindruckend
appointment	Termin
to look forward to	sich freuen auf

Übung 1

Vervollständigen Sie die Tabelle.

Nouns	Verbs
application	____________
purchasing	____________
manager	____________
____________	meet
____________	discuss
____________	interview
____________	confirm

Übung 2

Übersetzen Sie die 14 Wörter von Übung 1 ins Deutsche.

Nouns	Verbs
____________	____________
____________	____________
____________	____________
____________	____________
____________	____________
____________	____________
____________	____________

Übung 3

Vervollständigen Sie die Sätze mit Wörtern aus dem Brief.

1 Please ________________ an appointment to see me next week.

2 I hope 2 o'clock on Wednesday is ________________ for you.

3 His work is very ________________ – we ought to pay him more.

4 She has applied for the ________________ of personnel manager.

5 Mr Ashcroft is the purchasing ________________.

6 Ms Collins is the ________________ manager.

7 The letter begins "Dear Miss Grayson" and finishes "Yours ________________".

8 Miss Grayson has sent a letter and a ________________ ________________.

9 Miss Grayson will ________________ Ms Collins' secretary to confirm the appointment.

B An interview

Miss Grayson ist gerade in einem Vorstellungsgespräch bei Maddison Industries.

Ms Collins: Well, Miss Grayson, your qualifications are excellent. You haven't had much experience yet, have you?

Miss Grayson: Not really. I've been working for my present employer for a year and a half.

Mr Ashcroft: Could you tell us why you're leaving your job, Miss Grayson?

Miss Grayson: Certainly. Firstly, I would like a position with more responsibility. Secondly, I think I could earn more, and the conditions you're offering are good. And I live very close to here – that would mean less travelling time. At the moment I'm spending a lot on bus fares, too.

MS COLLINS	If you accept our offer of employment, we will pay you a starting salary of £12,000 a year. We also have good fringe benefits for our employees like private health insurance and an inexpensive cafeteria.
MISS GRAYSON	What about working hours?
MS COLLINS	Monday to Friday, 9 a.m. to 5.30 p.m., with an hour for lunch. We also have a short break for coffee in the morning and tea in the afternoon.
MR ASHCROFT	But occasionally I have to ask my secretary to stay a little later. We pay extra for overtime, of course.
MISS GRAYSON	That sounds very attractive. When will I know whether you'll offer me the job?
MS COLLINS	We've already decided. When can you take up the position?
MISS GRAYSON	I have to give a month's notice, so I could start on 1 October. And thank you!
MR ASHCROFT	Thank you, Miss Grayson. We'll send you our offer in writing, and hope you'll accept it.

Wendungen und Begriffe

experience	Erfahrung	*fringe benefit*	zusätzliche Leistung
fare	Fahrgeld	*health insurance*	Krankenversicherung
offer of employment	Beschäftigungsangebot	*inexpensive*	preisgünstig
		notice	Kündigungsfrist

Übung 4

Finden Sie für diese Sätze die entsprechenden Ausdrücke im Dialog.

1 Time which people spend going to and from work.

___

2 Money which people receive every month for working.

___

3 Things – in addition to money – which companies give people who work for them.

___

4 All the people who work for a company.

___

5 The time people spend at work.

____

6 Time which you spend at work after regular working hours.

____

7 To start a new job.

____

8 Telling your employer that you are going to leave.

____

Übung 5

Vervollständigen Sie diese Sätze mit Wörtern aus dem Vorstellungsgespräch.

1 You have an hour for lunch and two other ____________ every day.

2 Lunch in the cafeteria only costs £2 – it's very ____________!

3 People often look for a new job so that they can ____________ more money.

4 We will put our offer ____________ and send it to you by post.

5 The offer is so ____________ that I am going to accept it.

6 When you apply for a job, you must mention your qualifications and ____________.

7 Employers should offer their staff good working ____________.

8 Private health ____________ is an example of a fringe benefit.

9 You will usually finish work at 5.30, but ____________ I will ask you to work later.

10 She has to go to work by bus, and ____________ are expensive.

11 Miss Grayson was pleased when they ____________ her a job.

12 She does not do ____________ very often, but she always gets paid for these extra hours.

Übung 6

Vervollständigen Sie die Sätze mit Hilfe der vorgegebenen Ausdrücke.

offer you the position of • take up the position on • starting salary • fringe benefits • working hours • overtime • hope you will accept

1 Sometimes we have to work ______________________ in the evening.

2 Our ______________________ include free lunches.

3 Can you ______________________ 1 October?

4 We are pleased to ______________________ purchasing manager with our company.

5 Your ______________________ will be $25,000.

6 We ______________________ our offer.

7 Our ______________________ are from 9 a.m. to 5.30 p.m.

Übung 7

Bilden Sie sinnvolle Sätze, indem Sie die beiden Satzhälften einander zuordnen.

1 She wants a position	a because the company pays overtime.
2 I can't start work next month	b when would I begin?
3 Travelling into London every day	c with more responsibility.
4 If I take the job	d you must mention qualifications and experience.
5 Everything about this job is great	e because I have to give three months' notice
6 I'm happy about doing extra work	f is expensive and takes a lot of time.
7 If you apply for a new job,	g but the money is a problem.

Hotels and meals 10

A Hotels

Fletcher Industries hält die jährliche Verkaufskonferenz in verschiedenen europäischen Städten ab. Mr Peter Lomax, der PR-Direktor des Hotels, führt den leitenden Direktor von Fletcher Industries durch das Haus.

'Welcome to Graf Zeppelin, Miss Glover. As you can see, we have a large reception area with plenty of sofas, armchairs and tables. There are receptionists, porters and security men on duty around the clock. We have safety deposit boxes here, so your staff's valuables will be perfectly safe. Our souvenir shop, travel agency and car-hire desk are on this side of the area.

Over there is one of our four bars, which are open from 11 a.m. until midnight. The others are on the first, second and third floors. By the way, if you want a drink after midnight, we have twenty-four hour room service. 'Happy hour' – two drinks for the price of one – is from six to seven. There are also two restaurants, one here on the ground floor and the other on the third. Room service will serve you light refreshments – snacks and drinks – at any time, day or night.

Shall we look at a room? ... This is one of our hundred and twenty twin-bedded rooms. We also have a number of single and double rooms. All rooms have telephones, minibars and cable television. Naturally, they all have private bathrooms with toilets, baths and showers.

Now, let's continue talking over a drink. Which bar would you like to see?'

Wendungen und Begriffe

porter	Portier	*safety deposit box*	Hotelsafe
security man	Sicherheitsmann	*valuables*	Wertsachen, Wertgegenstände
on duty	im Dienst sein	*light refreshment*	(kleine) Erfrischung

Übung 1

Sie wohnen im Hotel Graf Zeppelin. Vervollständigen Sie die Antworten mit Hilfe des Textes.

1 A friend is going to collect you and take you to the theatre. Where will you wait for him?

In the ______________________________.

2 You need someone to help you take your luggage to your room. Who do you ask?

One of the ______________________________.

3 Where do you leave your passport, airline ticket and money?

In one of the ______________________________.

4 Where can you buy presents for your family and friends?

At the ______________________________.

5 You need a car for a week. Where do you rent it?

At the ______________________________.

6 You feel hungry in the middle of the night. What do you do?

Call ______________________________.

7 You want a room on your own. What sort of room do you book?

A ______________________________.

Übung 2

Ordnen Sie folgende Begriffe den passenden Oberbegriffen zu.

sofas • restaurants • beds • souvenir shop • bars • armchairs • receptionists • tables • porters • travel agency

Furniture	Staff	Hotel amenities
______	______	______
______	______	______
______	______	______
______	______	______

Übung 3

Vervollständigen Sie diese Postkarte mit passenden Ausdrücken aus dem Text.

Monday

We feel very safe at the Graf Zeppelin, because there are ________[1] on duty 24 hours a day. We leave our valuables in our ________[2], so we know they are safe. Our room is very comfortable, too. Having ________[3] is wonderful – we've got a choice of 48 different programmes.

As you know, Jim likes a drink, and there are four ________[4] here! He really likes ________[5] when drinks are half price. Sometimes he gets thirsty in the middle of the night, so he calls ________[6] when he's emptied the ________[7] in his room!

There are all sorts of other facilities here, like a souvenir ________[8] and a travel ________[9], and we're very happy. Jim says "Cheers" to all of you.

See you next week.

Best wishes Sarah

Mr
15
Ma
MA

B Meals

Starters

Soup of the day	$3.00
French onion soup	$4.50
Shrimp cocktail	$5.75
Paté maison	$4.75
Smoked salmon	$7.50

Main dishes

Grilled fillet of plaice	$10.00
Poached trout	$10.00
Chicken Kiev	$10.50
Roast duck	$11.25
T-bone steak	$12.00
Fillet steak	$13.50

All main dishes are served with the vegetables of the day and a choice of boiled, new or French fried potatoes.

Desserts

Apple pie and cream	$3.50
Chocolate mousse	$4.00
Pastries	$4.00
Ice-cream	$3.00

Coffees

American	$2.00
Espresso	$3.00
Cappuccino	$3.00
Irish	$6.00

For our selection of beers, wines and spirits, please ask to see the wine list.

GUEST A table for two, please.
HEAD WAITER Do you have a reservation?
GUEST Yes. In the name of Sarah Glover.

(At the table)
WAITER Would you like an aperitif before your dinner, sir?
GUEST Yes, please. A gin and tonic for the lady and a Campari soda for me.

(Later)
WAITER May I take your order, sir?
GUEST Poached trout for my friend, and fillet steak for me, please.
WAITER Would you like a starter?
GUEST No, thank you. We'll just have the main course.
WAITER How would you like your steak done? Medium?
GUEST No. Rare, please, for me.
WAITER How about potatoes?
GUEST New potatoes with the fish and French fries with the steak, please.
WAITER Would you like some wine?
GUEST Yes. Bring us the wine list, please.

WAITER	Can I interest you in a dessert?
GUEST	No, thank you. Just two coffees, please.
WAITER	Black or white, sir?
GUEST	One white and one black, please. And two double brandies.

(Later)

GUEST	Could I have the bill, please?

Wendungen und Begriffe

poached trout	gedünstete Forelle	*pastries*	(Blätterteig)gebäck
boiled	gekocht	*rare*	„englisch"

Übung 4

Unterstreichen Sie den Begriff, der nicht in die Wortgruppe gehört und ersetzen Sie ihn durch ein passendes Wort.

1	2	3	4
wine	cappuccino	T-bone steak	roast duck
gin	American	potatoes	apple pie
soup	fillet steak	poached trout	chocolate mousse
brandy	Irish	chicken Kiev	pastries
______________	______________	______________	______________

Übung 5

Vervollständigen Sie die Sätze mit dem richtigen Ausdruck (*kursiv* geschrieben).

1 I'd like *grilled/boiled* potatoes, please.
2 May I see the wine *list/menu*, please?
3 Two *black/rare* coffees, please.
4 I'd like my steak *rare/main*, please.
5 Would you like *a dessert/an aperitif* before we eat?
6 The *vegetables/potatoes* of the day are broccoli and carrots.
7 Would you like a *coffee/starter* before the main course?
8 That was a very good meal. Will you bring us the *menu/bill*, please?
9 The wine list includes a good *menu/selection* of French wines.
10 We must *serve/reserve* a table for this evening.

Übung 6

Sie befinden sich zusammen mit einem Freund/einer Freundin in einem Restaurant. Vervollständigen Sie den Dialog unter Verwendung der Begriffe aus der Karte und den kurzen Unterhaltungen.

WAITER Would you like a drink before your meal?

YOU Yes, please. ______________________________

______________________________[1]. And we'd like to order now.

WAITER Certainly. A starter?

YOU Yes. ______________________________[2] for me and ______________________________

______________________________[3] for my friend.

WAITER And the main course? I can recommend the fillet steaks.

YOU Good. Two ______________________________[4].

WAITER How would you like them done?

YOU ______________________________[5] for my friend and ______________________________[6]

for me, please.

WAITER What sort of potatoes would you like?

YOU ______________________________[7].

WAITER Would you like some wine?

YOU No, thank you. Two ______________________________[8].

(Later)

WAITER Would you like to order ______________________________[9]?

YOU No, thank you. Two coffees, please. ______________________________[10] for my friend and

______________________________[11]. And two ______________________________[12].

(Later)

YOU Waiter! Will you bring us ______________________________[13]?

WAITER Yes, of course.

Transport and packaging 11

A Instructions

Winos PLC

19.2.199.

Dear Madam/Sir

INSTRUCTIONS FOR PACKING AND TRANSPORTING WINE

Unfortunately we have to inform you that we are not satisfied with your packaging. Your last delivery contained seven breakages. We also have to inform you that your last consignment arrived more than three weeks late. We would be most grateful if you could follow these instructions carefully.

Wrap the bottles individually in strong wrapping paper. Then pack them in plywood cases. The cases must contain dividers to separate the bottles from each other. Each case should contain 12 bottles. Close the lids firmly.

Then place the cases in strong wooden crates, 24 to a crate. Please line the crates with waterproof material. Secure the crates with metal bands. Mark them clearly with these warning signs:
HANDLE WITH CARE, THIS SIDE UP and FRAGILE.

Kindly airfreight future deliveries, and invoice us for the extra cost. Several recent consignments which were either sent by sea and rail or sea and road have arrived late, so we hope that airfreighting will solve this problem.

Thank you for your attention to these matters.

Yours faithfully
WINOS PLC
Joanna Sessions
Joanna Sessions
Chief Buyer

Wendungen und Begriffe

delivery	Lieferung	*lid*	Deckel
consignment	Sendung	*crate*	Kiste
grateful	dankbar	*to line*	ausschlagen, auskleiden
wrapping paper	Packpapier	*to secure*	befestigen, sichern
plywood	Sperrholz	*kindly*	bitte
case	Kasten	*to airfreight*	als Luftfracht verschicken/versenden
divider	Trennstreifen		

Übung 1

Vervollständigen Sie die Tabelle, indem Sie aus den Verben Substantive bilden.

Verbs	Nouns
satisfy	______________
break	______________
wrap	______________
pack	______________
contain	______________
divide	______________
instruct	______________
deliver	______________
airfreight	______________

Übung 2

Benutzen Sie nun diese Substantive zur Vervollständigung dieser Sätze.

1 The last consignment was not packed to our ______________.

2 The damage done was due to bad ______________ – please use stronger materials in future.

3 ______________ the goods in strong paper is very important.

4 Please mark all future ______________ with the word “FRAGILE”.

5 We recommend the use of ____________________ to separate the bottles.

6 There were twelve ____________________ in your last consignment of glassware.

7 ____________________ is a faster but more expensive way of transporting goods.

8 We hope our packaging ____________________ will lead to fewer breakages in future.

Übung 3

Finden Sie im Beschwerdebrief Synonyme für folgende Begriffe:

1 previous ____________________

2 delivery ____________________

3 one by one ____________________

4 securely ____________________

5 please ____________________

6 send by air ____________________

7 additional ____________________

8 by ship ____________________

9 by truck ____________________

Übung 4

Übersetzen Sie ins Deutsche.

Please follow these instructions carefully. Pack the articles individually in strong wooden cases. Place the cases in a crate and make sure the lids are firmly closed. Mark the crate "Handle with care" and send it to us by air.

____

____

____

____

____

B Customs

Dieser Dialog findet beim Zoll auf einem internationalen Flughafen statt.

Customs officer	Have you anything to declare, madam?
Mrs Wainright	Only personal effects, a little alcohol and a few cigarettes, and these two packages.
Customs officer	How much alcohol and how many cigarettes?
Mrs Wainright	Two bottles of spirits, a bottle of wine and two hundred cigarettes.
Customs officer	Your duty-free allowance is one bottle of spirits and one of wine. I have to charge you duty on the other bottle of spirits. Will you open your suitcase, please? ... Thank you. When and where did you buy this camera?
Mrs Wainright	Last week, in Japan.
Customs officer	But you didn't declare it. I'll have to charge you duty, and you'll have to pay a fine. Open your handbag, please. ... Six watches!
Mrs Wainright	They're presents for my grandchildren. I didn't think presents were subject to duty.
Customs officer	But they are. How much foreign currency are you carrying?
Mrs Wainright	About $25,000. It's in my briefcase.
Customs officer	Fill in this currency declaration form, please. Then we'll go to my office and do the rest of the paperwork. I'm afraid you've tried to bring goods into the country illegally. You may be guilty of smuggling.
Mrs Wainright	No, officer! I'm an innocent old lady!

Übung 5

Finden Sie die Antonyme.

1 a lot of ____________________

2 next week ____________________

3 legally ____________________

4 guilty ____________________

Übung 6

Nennen Sie die Oberbegriffe.

1 money used in other countries ____________________

2 what you may bring into a country without paying tax ____________________

3 money you pay as a punishment ____________________

4 importing goods illegally ____________________

5 whisky, brandy, gin, etc. ____________________

6 to say what taxable goods you have with you ____________________

7 things which belong to us, like clothes ____________________

8 tax paid to customs ____________________

Übung 7

Bilden Sie sinnvolle Sätze, indem Sie die beiden Satzhälften einander zuordnen.

1 Wines and spirits	a to declare?
2 Customs charge	b to import restricted items.
3 If you break the law,	c of smuggling.
4 You need a permit	d duty on some goods.
5 Have you anything	e are subject to duty.
6 You are guilty	f you may have to pay a fine.

12 Production

A Industry

Hier finden Sie einen Überblick über die Industrie. Es werden verschiedene Industriezweige, ihre Aufgabengebiete und typische Arbeitsbedingungen in einer Fabrik dargestellt.

Countries produce goods. For example, miners extract coal from the earth and dairies provide us with milk. Volkswagen and Mercedes-Benz manufacture motor vehicles. Construction companies need, for instance, things like bricks, floorboards and windows in order to build houses with them.

These are examples of what happens in industry. Primary industries like agriculture, forestry and oil drilling, take raw materials from their sources. Then secondary industries, such as shipbuilding and the furniture industry, turn these raw materials into semi-finished and finished goods. So we can define the word industry as "extracting raw materials from their sources and turning them into finished goods".

Manufacturing takes place in factories and workshops. A factory is a large building which contains machines and other equipment.

Lots of factories produce goods twenty-four hours a day. The workers work in shifts: the morning shift may start at 6 a.m., for example, and finish at 2 p.m. Then comes the afternoon shift, from 2 o'clock in the afternoon until 10 o'clock in the evening. Finally there is the night shift, from late in the evening until early the next morning. The person in charge of each shift is the shift supervisor. He/she has an office in the factory, and he/she is responsible to the production manager.

Some factories, in the car industry for example, are automated. They are controlled by computers, and they use robots to produce articles. This means that the number of workers is very small.

Wendungen und Begriffe

miner	Bergarbeiter	*floorboard*	Diele
to extract	fördern	*forestry*	Forstwirtschaft
dairy	Molkerei	*oil drilling*	Ölförderung
to manufacture	herstellen	*to turn sth into sth*	umwandeln
brick	Ziegelstein	*to control*	steuern

Übung 1

Vervollständigen Sie die Tabelle, indem Sie die zwei Industriezweige mit jeweils drei Beispielen angeben.

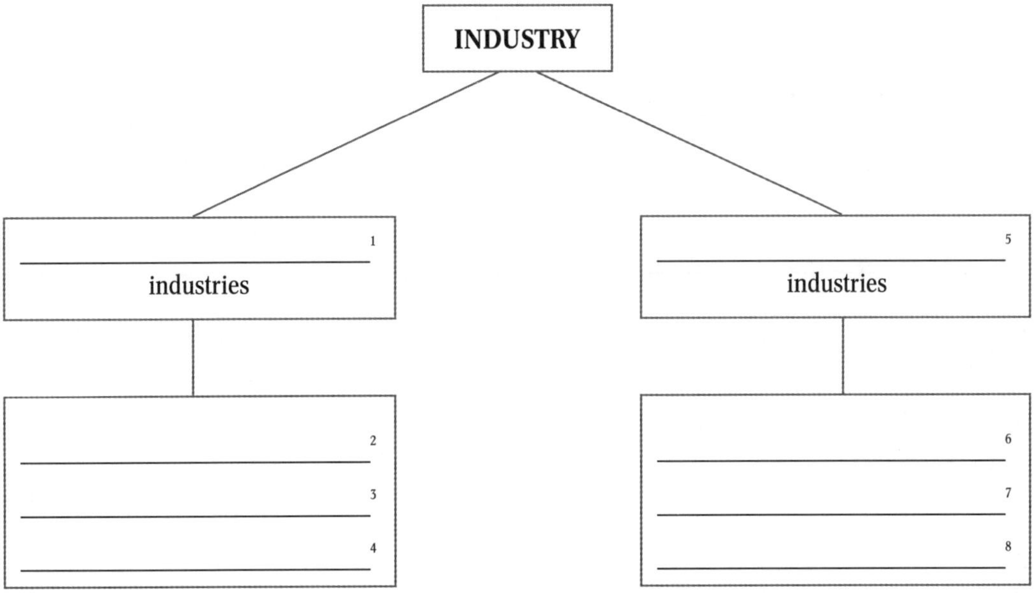

Übung 2

Vervollständigen Sie die Tabelle.

Nouns	Verbs
______________	produce
manufacturing	______________
______________	drill
______________	construct
______________	build
mining	______________
extraction	______________

Übung 3

Ordnen Sie diese Ausdrücke den richtigen Oberbegriffen zu.

office • car • construction • agriculture • production manager • finished goods • workers • housebuilding • workshop • shift supervisor • oil drilling • factory • dairy • computer

Activities	Places of work	People	Products
________	________	________	________
________	________	________	________
________	________	________	________
________	________	________	________

B Commerce

Dieser Text gibt einen Überblick über den Handel und die fünf dazugehörenden Bereiche.

When goods have been produced, they have to be sold. This is the business of commerce, which deals with selling products, paying for them and insuring and transporting them. So the five activities connected with commerce are trade, banking, warehousing, insurance and transport.

Trade means buying and selling. Banks handle cheques and other documents, and give credit to customers who need it. A warehouse is a large building where suppliers store goods until customers need them. Insurance companies cover goods against risks like fire and theft. And transport means moving goods from the seller to the buyer: this can be done by road, rail, sea or air.

Communications are an essential part of commerce. Nowadays people in business use the telephone and fax every day, and technology in this area is very advanced.

Wendungen und Begriffe

to be connected with	verbunden mit	*essential*	erforderlich, notwendig
		nowadays	heute, heutzutage
theft	Diebstahl	*advanced*	fortgeschritten, entwickelt

Übung 4

Beantworten Sie diese Fragen.

1 What is the business of commerce? ____________________

2 Which word means "exchanging goods for money"? ____________________

3 Which activity deals with cheques and lending money? ____________________

4 What is another word for "buyer"? ____________________

5 Where do sellers store goods before selling them to buyers? ____________________

6 Which activity covers risks? ____________________

Übung 5

Bilden Sie sinnvolle Sätze, indem Sie die beiden Satzhälften einander zuordnen.

1 Trade and transport	a covers goods against risks.
2 Customers often pay	b to buyers.
3 Production and industry	c in warehouses.
4 Goods are stored	d are parts of commerce.
5 Goods must be transported	e by cheque.
6 Insurance	f do not mean the same.

Übung 6

Vervollständigen Sie diese Sätze mit Wörtern aus dem Text. Achten Sie auf die richtige Form.

1 Goods are ________________ in factories.

2 They are ________________ in a warehouse until they are delivered to customers.

3 They are covered by ________________ against fire and theft.

4 They are ________________ to the customer by road, rail, sea or air.

5 Suppliers are often paid by ________________.

6 One of the functions of a bank is to give ________________ to customers.

Übung 7

Übersetzen Sie die Sätze ins Deutsche.

1 The five activities connected with commerce are trade, banking, warehousing, insurance and transport.

2 Trade means buying and selling.

3 Banks handle cheques and other documents, and give credit to customers who need it.

4 Transport means moving goods from the seller to the buyer: this can be done by road, rail, sea or air.

5 Nowadays people in business use the telephone and fax every day.

Lösungen

1 The office

Übung 1

1	keeps	5	stores
2	belongs	6	contains
3	types	7	finds
4	shows	8	needs

Übung 2

Furniture: desks, filing cabinets, chairs, tables
Stationery: envelopes, pens, paper, pencils
Equipment: printers, computer

Übung 3

1 Miss Brown's desk is on the right of the picture.
2 The filing cabinets are beside the window.
3 The safe is in the corner of the office.
4 There are two chairs in front of Mr Dawson's desk.
5 The table is below the window.
6 The sales manager keeps money in the safe.
7 Miss Brown's message pad is on top of her desk.
8 Miss Brown has two drawers on the right of her desk.

Übung 4

1 sometimes, occasionally
2 in charge of
3 customers
4 overseas, abroad
5 staff
6 agent
7 appointments

Übung 5

occasionally	computer	store
often	keyboard	contain
usually	disk	keep
sometimes	monitor	hold

2 The company

Übung 1

car park – factory – floor – secretary

Übung 2

1	canteen	6	floor
2	marketing	7	production
3	train/bus	8	loading bay
4	first-aid room	9	car park
5	board room		

Übung 3

1	situated	3	make
2	staff	4	products

Übung 4

1	a long way away	3	female
2	small	4	unload

Übung 5

1 floor
2 factory
3 employees/staff, canteen
4 car park
5 load/unload, bay
6 raw
7 buildings
8 department, offices
9 meet, board
10 managing, secretary

Übung 6

1	Board	9	customers
2	responsible	10	buys
3	decisions	11	after
4	appoint	12	runs
5	runs	13	goods
6	charge	14	head
7	accountant	15	sales
8	invoices		

Übung 7

1 The accounts department
2 The managing director
3 The Board of Directors
4 The personnel department
5 The production department
6 The marketing department
7 The purchasing department
8 The marketing department

Übung 8
My office is on the ground floor of the factory building. I am in charge of the production department, and I make decisions about the goods which the company produces. I am responsible to the managing director. I work with the marketing manager, who advertises and sells the goods we make. I also work with the chief accountant, who pays for the raw materials we need.

3 Secretarial duties

Übung 1

Nouns	Verbs
apology	apologize
flight	fly
reservation	reserve
production	produce
sales	sell
manager	manage
meeting	meet
introduction	introduce
discussion	discuss
invitation	invite

Übung 2
1 produce
2 invitation
3 discussion
4 meeting
5 reserve
6 fly
7 apologize
8 manage
9 sell
10 introduction

Übung 3
coffee - reservation - later

Übung 4
1 breakfast
2 secretary
3 coffee
4 lunch
5 managing director
6 dinner
7 reservation

Übung 5
1 Did you have a good flight? - Fine, thanks.
2 Are you free tomorrow? - Yes, I am.
3 Can I get you a coffee? - Yes, please, that'd be very nice.
4 Do you know what my programme is?- I'm afraid not.
5 How about discussing this over lunch? - Good idea. Let's do that.
6 Is this your first trip to Berlin? - Yes, it is actually.

Übung 6
1 memo
2 reps
3 a.m.
4 AOB
5 ASAP

Übung 7
1 Verschiedenes, Sonstiges
2 sobald wie möglich
3 Vertreter
4 morgens

Übung 8
1 representatives
2 Sales
3 Department
4 attend
5 at
6 on
7 at
8 conference
9 items
10 agenda
11 Minutes of the last meeting
12 Sales figures for last year
13 Our plans for the second half of this year
14 AOB
15 Secretary

Übung 9
1 Is there any other business?
2 There are six items on the agenda.
3 All the representatives will attend the meeting.
4 He is in Germany on business.
5 A secretary takes the minutes.
6 Please send the memo as soon as possible.

Übung 10
1 Gibt es noch etwas?
2 Es stehen sechs Punkte auf der Tagesordnung.
3 Alle Vertreter werden an der Besprechung teilnehmen.
4 Er ist in Deutschland auf Geschäftsreise.
5 Ein(e) Sekretär(in) führt Protokoll.
6 Bitte schicken Sie das Memo sobald wie möglich.

Übung 11
telephone call *(All the others are written down.)*
Board of Directors *(More than one person.)*
conference room *(This is where the meeting is held, all the others are to do with the meeting itself.)*
write *(You can hold, plan, attend and arrange a meeting.)*

4 Telephoning

Übung 1
1 Dialling
2 code
3 country code
4 area code
5 customer's
6 international operator
7 transfer charge
8 personal
9 services

Übung 2
1 quick
2 easy
3 abroad
4 more
5 can

Übung 3
1 We must look up the right area code.
2 Special services are things like personal calls or collect calls.
3 IDD lets us telephone almost 200 countries.
4 First we dial the international code.
5 Country codes are listed in the telephone book.
6 We find area codes under country entries.

Übung 4
1 Könnte ich mit ... sprechen?
2 Leider ...
3 Kann ich ihm/ihr eine Nachricht übermitteln?
4 Es tut mir leid, ...
5 Könnten Sie mir das bitte buchstabieren?
6 Selbstverständlich.
7 Vorname
8 "a" großgeschrieben
9 Nachname
10 "e" kleingeschrieben
11 Es ist dringend.
12 Ich danke Ihnen für Ihren Anruf.

Übung 5
-

Übung 6
TELEPHONIST Fletcher Industries, good morning.
UTA HÜBNER May I speak to Miss Glover, please?
TELEPHONIST I'm sorry, but Miss Glover is in Birmingham. Can I take a message?
UTA HÜBNER This is Uta Hübner of Götz Metall, Berlin.
TELEPHONIST Would you spell that, please?
UTA HÜBNER Certainly. First name capital U, t, a. Last name capital H, u, e, b, n, e, r.
TELEPHONIST Thank you. And your message, please?
UTA HÜBNER It's not urgent. I'll call again next week.
TELEPHONIST Thank you for calling. Goodbye.

5 Travelling

Übung 1
Nouns	**Verbs**
fax	fax
reservation	reserve
departure	depart
driver	drive
confirmation	confirm
arrangement	arrange
call	call
booking	book

Übung 2
1 economy class
2 return
3 reservation
4 late afternoon flight
5 seats available

Übung 3
1 Luxus-
2 Touristenklasse
3 Abendessen
4 Nacht-
5 Mittagessen

Übung 4
Hotel classifications: five-star, first class, luxury
Meals: breakfast, dinner, lunch
Timings of airline flights: late afternoon, early morning, late night
Types of airline seat: business class, economy class

Übung 5
Luggage: bag, briefcase, suitcase
Documents: visa, landing card, passport
Drinks: spirits, wine, beer
Currencies: mark, dollar, franc
Airport facilities: restrooms, bar, taxi rank, restaurant, bureau de change

Übung 6
1 immigration official
2 customs officials
3 dangerous drugs
4 weapons
5 magazines
6 spirits
7 duty

Übung 7
1 directly, without delay
2 retain
3 return
4 items
5 unlimited
6 prohibited
7 duty-free

Übung 8

1 Airport
2 passport
3 Immigration
4 luggage
5 baggage reclaim
6 duty
7 duty-free
8 other
9 amounts

6 Buying

Übung 1

1 more
2 larger, bigger
3 new
4 in the past
5 later
6 the end of

Übung 2

1 unpopular
2 dissatisfied
3 impossible
4 dislike
5 displeased

Übung 3

Nouns	**Verbs**
information	inform
enquiry	enquire
guarantee	guarantee
delivery	deliver
stocks	stock
allowance	allow
need	need
offer	offer
advice	advise
discussion	discuss

Übung 4

1 enquire, information, discuss
2 deliver, stocks
3 guarantee
4 need, information/advice
5 allow/offer
6 need, stock
7 advise
8 discussion, need

Übung 5

1 need
2 guarantee
3 stocks
4 enquiring
5 advice
6 allowance
7 discuss
8 offer
9 deliver
10 inform

Übung 6

Our prices are very competitive, and we allow large discounts. The quality of the products is high, and our customers are very satisfied. The goods will be sent by special delivery by the end of next week.

Übung 7

1 I can afford a new house.
2 Some cars are more expensive than others.
3 We are worried about delivery times.
4 Some suppliers ask customers to pay cash at once.
5 If you are lucky, you can find goods on special offer.
6 I am paying for my computer on hire purchase terms.
7 I will pay half the price now, and the balance over six months.
8 We normally pay for merchandise/products in the shop.
9 Most buyers are price-conscious and quality-conscious.
10 When you purchase large quantities, you will receive a discount.

Übung 8

customer – manufacturers – after-sales service – save

Übung 9

Lösungsvorschläge

1 She was the first customer to come into the shop this morning.
2 If the product is faulty, return it to the manufacturers.
3 We sometimes have to pay a little more for after-sales service.
4 We must save money, so that we can afford a holiday.

Übung 10

1 I cannot afford to pay a lot of money.
2 Some suppliers ask for cash, but others allow credit.
3 We guarantee the article for a year.
4 They are talking about terms of payment.
5 A large house is more expensive than a small one.
6 We are offering this model at DM 1,000.
7 All customers should be price-conscious.
8 Buyers can choose between different suppliers.
9 We have several models in stock.
10 If you shop carefully, you can save money.

7 Selling

Übung 1

1 buy	6 cash
2 save	7 department store
3 price	8 deliver
4 goods	9 discount
5 sale	10 deposit

Übung 2

At our annual bargain sale we offer our customers a wide range of goods at unbelievably low prices. You can buy everything at sale prices: we give huge discounts. And we deliver your purchases to your home.

Übung 3

1 bargain	4 save
2 deliver	5 cash and carry
3 articles	6 deposit

Übung 4

1 orange growers	5 consumers
2 a wholesaler	6 greengrocers
3 retailers	7 department stores
4 supermarkets	8 to make a profit

Übung 5

Group 1: consumers, wholesalers, producers, retailers
Group 2: chain stores, supermarkets, department stores, greengrocers
Group 3: cover costs, make a loss, make a profit, sell for 25p
Group 4: products, foodstuffs

Übung 6

Verbs	Nouns
consume	consumer
retail	retailer
produce	producer
grow	grower
sell	seller
buy	buyer

8 Banking and payments

Übung 1

1 safe	5 transfer
2 cheques	6 deposit
3 interest	7 statement
4 currency	8 security

Übung 2

1 borrow	5 lend
2 lend	6 borrow
3 lend	7 lend
4 borrow	8 borrow(ed)

Übung 3

Money: salary, cash, savings, currency
Documents: cheque, statement, bills
Banking services: cash card, loan, deposits, withdrawals

Übung 4

Nouns	Verbs
advice	advise
loan	lend
service	serve, service
savings	save
employer	employ
earnings	earn
payment	pay
deposit	deposit
withdrawal	withdraw
transfer	transfer

Übung 5

1 quarterly	6 balance
2 invoice	7 cash
3 statement	8 salaries
4 unit price	9 wages
5 insurance costs	10 fees

Übung 6

transactions – staff – credit – unit price

Übung 7

1 people in business	3 money
2 documents	4 expenses

Übung 8

1 Statements are sent every three months.
2 Most customers pay by cheque.
3 We grant credit to some customers.
4 An invoice lists the goods and prices.

5 Salaries are paid monthly.
6 The final figure on a statement is the balance.
7 Invoices are sent with orders.
8 Transactions are credits and debits.

9 Applications and interviews

Übung 1

Nouns	**Verbs**
application	apply
purchasing	purchase
manager	manage
meeting	meet
discussion	discuss
interview	interview
confirmation	confirm

Übung 2

Bewerbung	bewerben
Einkauf	einkaufen
Manager	führen, leiten, verwalten
Sitzung, Versammlung	treffen
Diskussion	diskutieren
Vorstellungsgespräch	interviewen, befragen
Bestätigung	bestätigen

Übung 3

1 make
2 convenient
3 impressive
4 post
5 manager
6 personnel
7 sincerely
8 curriculum vitae
9 telephone

Übung 4

1 travelling time
2 salary
3 fringe benefits
4 employees
5 working hours
6 overtime
7 to take up a position
8 giving notice

Übung 5

1 breaks
2 inexpensive
3 earn
4 in writing
5 attractive
6 experience
7 conditions
8 insurance
9 occasionally
10 fares
11 offered
12 overtime

Übung 6

1 overtime
2 fringe benefits
3 take up the position on
4 offer you the position of
5 starting salary
6 hope you will accept
7 working hours

Übung 7

1 She wants a position with more responsibility.
2 I can't start work next month because I have to give three months' notice.
3 Travelling into London every day is expensive and takes a lot of time.
4 If I take the job when would I begin?
5 Everything about this job is great but the money is a problem.
6 I'm happy about doing extra work because the company pays overtime.
7 If you apply for a new job, you must mention qualifications and experience.

10 Hotels and meals

Übung 1

1 In the reception area.
2 One of the porters.
3 In one of the safety deposit boxes.
4 At the souvenir shop.
5 At the car-hire desk.
6 Call room service.
7 A single room.

Übung 2

Furniture: sofas, beds, armchairs, tables
Staff: receptionists, porters
Hotel amenities: restaurants, souvenir shop, bars, travel agency

Übung 3

1 security men
2 safety deposit box
3 cable television
4 bars
5 Happy hour
6 room service
7 minibar
8 shop
9 agency

Übung 4
soup – fillet steak – potatoes – roast duck
Lösungsvorschlag
beer – espresso – roast duck – ice-cream

Übung 5

1	boiled	6	vegetables
2	list	7	starter
3	black	8	bill
4	rare	9	selection
5	an aperitif	10	reserve

Übung 6
Lösungsvorschlag

WAITER	Would you like a drink before your meal?
YOU	Yes, please. A whisky and soda for the lady and a beer for me. And we'd like to order now.
WAITER	Certainly. A starter?
YOU	Yes. A shrimp cocktail for me and smoked salmon for my friend.
WAITER	And the main course? I can recommend the fillet steaks.
YOU	Good. Two fillet steaks, please.
WAITER	How would you like them done?
YOU	Medium for my friend and rare for me, please.
WAITER	What sort of potatoes would you like?
YOU	French fries, please.
WAITER	Would you like some wine?
YOU	No, thank you. Two beers.
(Later)	
WAITER	Would you like to order dessert?
YOU	No, thank you. Two coffees, please. Cappuccino for my friend and American for me. And two brandies, please.
(Later)	
YOU	Waiter! Will you bring us the bill, please?
WAITER	Yes, of course.

11 Transport and packaging

Übung 1

Verbs	Nouns
satisfy	satisfaction
break	breakage
wrap	wrapping
pack	packaging, package
contain	container, contents
divide	divider
instruct	instruction
deliver	delivery
airfreight	airfreight

Übung 2

1	satisfaction	5	dividers
2	packaging	6	breakages
3	Wrapping	7	Airfreight, Airfreighting
4	deliveries	8	instructions

Übung 3

1	last	6	airfreight
2	consignment	7	extra
3	individually	8	by sea
4	firmly	9	by road
5	kindly		

Übung 4
Befolgen Sie diese Anweisungen bitte sorgfältig. Verpacken Sie die Artikel einzeln in stabile Holzkästen. Verpacken Sie die Kästen in einer Kiste, die Sie fest verschließen. Kennzeichnen Sie die Kiste „Vorsicht – zerbrechlich" und schicken Sie sie uns per Flugzeug.

Übung 5
1 a little, a few
2 last week
3 illegally
4 innocent

Übung 6

1	foreign currency	5	spirits
2	duty-free allowance	6	to declare
3	a fine	7	personal effects
4	smuggling	8	(customs) duty

Übung 7
1 Wines and spirits are subject to duty.
2 Customs charge duty on some goods.
3 If you break the law, you may have to pay a fine.
4 You need a permit to import restricted items.
5 Have you anything to declare?
6 You are guilty of smuggling.

12 Production

Übung 1

1	Primary	5	Secondary
2	Agriculture	6	Shipbuilding
3	Forestry	7	Furniture
4	Oil drilling	8	Construction, Car manufacturing

Übung 2

Nouns	Verbs
production, produce	produce
manufacturing	manufacture
drilling	drill
construction	construct
building	build
mining	mine
extraction	extract

Übung 3

Activities: construction, agriculture, housebuilding, oil drilling
Places of work: office, workshop, factory, dairy
People: production manager, workers, shift supervisor
Products: car, finished goods, computer

Übung 4

1 selling products
2 trade
3 banking
4 customer
5 in warehouses
6 insurance

Übung 5

1 Trade and transport are parts of commerce.
2 Customers often pay by cheque.
3 Production and industry do not mean the same.
4 Goods are stored in warehouses.
5 Goods must be transported to buyers.
6 Insurance covers goods against risks.

Übung 6

1 produced
2 stored
3 insurance
4 transported
5 cheque
6 credit

Übung 7

1 Die fünf Tätigkeiten, die mit dem Geschäftsleben verbunden sind, sind Handel, Bankwesen, Lagerwirtschaft, Versicherung und Transport.
2 Handel bedeutet Kaufen und Verkaufen.
3 Die Banken bearbeiten Schecks und andere Dokumente und vergeben Kredite an Kunden, die sie brauchen.
4 Transport bedeutet, Güter vom Verkäufer zum Käufer zu bewegen: das kann per Straße, per Schiene oder auf dem Wasser- oder Luftweg geschehen.
5 Heutzutage benutzen die Geschäftsleute jeden Tag Telefon und Fax.

Quellennachweis

Fotos:
Bavaria Fotoagentur, Düsseldorf S. 8, 42, 45 (unten links)
Comstock S. 53, 68 (links)
David Graham, London S. 16, 33 (oben rechts, unten links), 66
Hotel Graf Zeppelin, Stuttgart S. 57 (alle)
Image Bank, Berlin S. 68 (oben rechts, unten rechts)
J. Allan Cash, London S. 45 (oben rechts)
ZEFA S. 68 (mitte rechts)

Illustrationen: **Pennant, London** S. 5, 6, 10